THE
GRANTWRITER'S
START-UP KIT
WORKBOOK

■ ■ ■ ■ ■

D1298156

THE
GRANTWRITER'S
START-UP KIT
WORKBOOK

A BEGINNER'S GUIDE
TO GRANT PROPOSALS

© Successful Images, Inc.

Special Thanks to
Carole Nugent, Tom Ezell, and Marina Pavlov
of the Florida Association of Nonprofits (FANO)
FANO

JOSSEY-BASS
A Wiley Company
www.josseybass.com

Published by

JOSSEY-BASS
A Wiley Company
989 Market Street
San Francisco, CA 94103-1741

www.josseybass.com

Jossey-Bass books and products are available through most bookstores. To contact Jossey-Bass directly, call (888) 378-2537, fax to (800) 605-2665, or visit our website at www.josseybass.com.

Substantial discounts on bulk quantities of Jossey-Bass books are available to corporations, professional associations, and other organizations. For details and discount information, contact the special sales department at Jossey-Bass.

ISBN: 0-7879-5232-X

All cases in this workbook are fictional. Any resemblance to real organizations or persons is coincidental.

We at Jossey-Bass strive to use the most environmentally sensitive paper stocks available to us. Our publications are printed on acid-free recycled stock whenever possible, and our paper always meets or exceeds minimum GPO and EPA requirements.

Interior design by Gene Crofts

PB Printing 10 9 8 7 6 5 4 3   FIRST EDITION

CONTENTS

■ ■ ■ ■

FOREWORD

■ ■ ■ ■ ■

Today in America there are more than one million nonprofit organizations working for worthy causes. Each of these organizations is competing for the same nonprofit dollars. Even though it is true that there are more grants available today than ever before, the question remains, How can you help your organization get the money it deserves? The answer is simple: learn to write a successful grant proposal.

The *Grantwriter's Start-Up Kit* video and workbook are designed to help you start the process of writing a successful grant proposal for a foundation or other donor. Using the information and guidelines in this package can save time for both you and the foundation you apply to and ultimately produce better results for both you and the foundation.

In grantwriting, as in any worthwhile endeavor, knowledge is power. Before you create a proposal, it is vital that you know the foundation's purpose and priorities. Research what kinds of projects the foundation funds, and just as important, know what it does not fund. Become familiar with its deadlines, and learn the names of the key personnel. Successful proposals are complete and concise. Contrary to a popular impression, foundations do not weigh proposals—they read them.

Even if you have never written a grant proposal before, you can learn the skills you need to create a powerful proposal—a proposal that will be easily understood and so compelling it can persuade the funder to consider granting you the funds you seek. Only proposals that are well written, well documented, and well constructed make the funder's final cut.

The Grantwriter's Start-Up Kit video and workbook can be your first step toward creating a successful grant proposal of your own.

Creed C. Black
Past president and trustee
John S. and James L. Knight Foundation

HOW THIS WORKBOOK CAN HELP YOU

■ ■ ■ ■

Writing grant proposals can be a daunting and intimidating process. There are many opportunities to make mistakes or get derailed or discouraged. The key to staying on track and writing a good proposal the first time out is being prepared *before* you sit down to write the proposal.

The Grantwriter's Start-Up Kit guides you easily and thoroughly through the preparation stage, giving you the information and confidence you need to embark on the grantwriting journey. By watching the video you have taken the first step—learning about the key elements of the grant proposal and gaining invaluable insights from professionals in the field. This workbook takes you through the next step. It will help you start to think like a grantwriter and begin to gather the information you need as you deepen and reinforce the knowledge you gained from the video. The tools provided in this video and workbook will help you prepare to get foundation, corporation, and association grants.

In Part One, seven *start-up exercises* give you the opportunity to begin asking the questions and finding the answers essential to writing a proposal. They will help you translate your knowledge and passion for your cause into language that speaks to grantmakers. As you complete these exercises you will gather the information you need to move forward, think about what you need to write a proposal and how to go about getting it, and lay the foundation for writing the proposal. Part One also encourages you to think about the next steps and how you will move forward.

Part Two is your resource guide. It offers a quick review of the highlights of the video, gives you tips on each of the key elements of a grant proposal, provides a sample of each element, and outlines proposal strategy and structure. *The Grantwriter's Start-Up Kit* shows you one common proposal format. Keep in mind that there are others and that you will use the one that best suits your needs and the requirements of your potential funder.

The first steps presented here are often ignored by experienced grantwriters and novices alike. By watching the video and completing the exercises, you can streamline the process and avoid common mistakes. This means you will make the most of your time and resources when you sit down to write your proposal. After using both the video and the workbook, you and your organization will be well on the way to creating a professional grant proposal that deserves funding consideration.

PART 1

START-UP EXERCISES

This first part of this workbook contains seven start-up exercises. Each exercise has three parts. First, work through the *Activity* section of the exercise. Take your time, and don't worry about "right" answers. These activities are designed to get you thinking. You are not committed to any choices you make now, so feel free to experiment. Second, after you complete the activity, move on to *Thinking About Next Steps.* This section will guide you as you consider what your next logical steps should be. The steps will be different for different organizations and different situations. Third, consider the section *When You Are Ready to Move On,* which shows you how you will use the information you gathered in this start-up exercise when you sit down to write your proposal. This section is designed to help you see how the work you have done will be put to use in writing a proposal. Resource A, in the second part of this workbook, includes samples of key proposal elements. Whenever you want to see what the contents of a particular element look like, flip ahead to these samples.

EXERCISE 1

■

Identifying a Fundable Project or Program

■ ■ ■ ■

The first step in creating a successful grant proposal is to identify a potentially fundable project or program. This exercise will help you choose likely projects or programs, those that are both in line with your organization's mission and within your organization's reach.

■ *Activity*

1. Write down your organization's mission or purpose. If your organization does not have a clear mission, or if its mission is in flux, you will need to make sure it has settled on a clear mission before you begin seeking grants. (There are grants available specifically for organizations seeking to define their mission!)

2. Keeping your organization's mission in mind, write down five to ten ideas for programs or projects that the organization would like to do. They can be very similar or very different. They can be new ideas or ways to expand or continue existing programs. They should be ideas your organization is passionate about—things it can do to make a difference.

3. Note down how each of these ideas does or does not reflect your organization's mission. Eliminate those ideas that are not representative of the mission. As you consider these ideas in relation to the mission, you may want to discuss them with others in the organization.

4. Are any other organizations doing similar projects that might be considered competitive? List those organizations and projects here.

5. Might any other organizations provide opportunities for collaboration on one or more of the projects your organization is considering? List those organizations here.

6. Among the fundable ideas that fit your organization's mission, are there any that your organization cannot realistically accomplish? Eliminate these ideas. Which programs or projects can your organization realistically coordinate? Circle these ideas. These are your best prospects for a fundable project. Select two or three of these project ideas to carry forward for the rest of the start-up exercises.

THINKING ABOUT NEXT STEPS

Write down five to ten ideas for the steps your organization might take next. For example, now that you have identified some fundable projects, can they be shaped to be more in line with your organization's mission? Can your organization cooperate with organizations with similar programs? If an idea you really like does not reflect the organization's mission, can you find another organization that has a mission that *does* match the program and can you partner with it? What are the plans for motivating the board to support the fundable projects you have identified?

▨ WHEN YOU ARE READY TO MOVE ON

When you are ready to begin writing a grant proposal, present your ideas to key people in the organization, or to colleagues if you are a one-person shop, and get feedback. Compose a compelling statement about the fundable project—one that explains why the program is important. This statement will be the basis for your needs statement when you are ready to write that part of the proposal.

EXERCISE 2

PINPOINTING THE NEED
YOUR PROJECT WILL FILL
OR THE PROBLEM IT WILL SOLVE

In this exercise you will identify the needs that your project ideas will fill or the problems they will solve. Here is where you begin to get specific. You also begin to think about how you will support your claim that the needs are real. When you talk about needs, talk about them from the community's rather than your organization's perspective. You are not asking for money because your organization needs money but because you want to fill a need in the community your organization serves.

ACTIVITY

1. Take the project and program ideas you selected in Exercise 1, and for each idea, write two or three sentences that clearly state the problem or need each program or project addresses.

2. Make a list of real-life stories you can tell to support your statement that these problems or needs exist. If you cannot think of any anecdotes, where can you go to find them?

3. Write down how you know that these problems or needs are not already addressed sufficiently by someone else.

4. Eventually you will need to document that each need or problem exists. To begin this process, list the leading newspapers, journals, and other publications in the field.

5. List the most credible authorities in the field. If you do not know their names, where can you go to find them out?

THINKING ABOUT NEXT STEPS

Write down five ideas for taking the next steps. For example, what resources (such as libraries or the Internet) can you use to begin the research process? Whom can you go to for help researching statistics and survey information? What will you do to document the need section of your proposal? You can use statistics, information from a survey or questionnaire, facts or predictions by authorities, interviews with client populations, projections, and quotations from newspapers.

WHEN YOU ARE READY TO MOVE ON

When you are ready to write the needs statement of your proposal, you can start with the needs you have identified here and with the documentation you have gathered. You will also want to make sure the statement meets the following criteria: it should be in sync with your organization's mission, jargon free, focused on filling a need within the community, and well documented. Moreover, fulfilling it should be within the scope of your organization.

E X E R C I S E 3

DEVELOPING CLEARLY STATED OBJECTIVES

■ ■ ■ ■ ■

In Exercise 2 you worked on establishing the need or problem, which explains *why* the program was or ought to be created. In this exercise you will explore the objectives, which explain (1) *what* the program will accomplish and (2) *what* impact that accomplishment will have on the community served. A good objective statement will be time sensitive and measurable. It usually will start with the word *to*. Here are some examples:

> To reduce student absenteeism in the school district by 20 percent over a three-year period

> To increase the number of pet adoptions in San Francisco by one hundred every year for five years

■ *ACTIVITY*

1. Write down the needs you identified in Exercise 2 for each of your two or three possible programs or projects.

2. You have now stated the needs, *why* your organization has created or wants to create the programs or projects. Now write down *what* each program or project intends to accomplish that will fulfill a need. Remember to begin your statements with the word *to*. Be specific.

3. Does each objective describe a benefit to the community served? If not, can you write down a way to reshape each objective that does not?

4. Does each objective tie in directly to the needs you have identified? If not, can you write down a way to reshape each objective that does not?

5. Is each objective specific, time sensitive, and measurable? If not, can you write down a way to reshape each objective that is not?

THINKING ABOUT NEXT STEPS

Write down some ideas for taking the next steps. For example, estimate how long will it take your organization to reach each objective. Start to identify who will be affected if you reach each objective. Make a list of the resources needed to reach each objective.

WHEN YOU ARE READY TO MOVE ON

When you are ready to write your proposal for a program, present the proposed objective or objectives to your organization's board and to others in your organization, or to your colleagues, and discuss whether or not the objectives are clear and realistic. Use the feedback you get to determine the best possible way to state the objectives. You will use this information to make the objectives section of your proposal powerful and compelling.

EXERCISE 4

■

ESTABLISHING THE METHODS YOU WILL USE

■ ■ ■ ■ ■

Now that you have determined the objectives for your organization's possible projects or programs, this exercise will help you consider *how* your organization will meet these objectives. In other words, what action will your organization take to solve the problems that have been identified?

■ ACTIVITY

1. Write down the objectives you identified in Exercise 3.

2. Think of all the steps and activities the organization will have to take to accomplish each objective. Make a detailed list of these steps and activities.

3. Using these steps and activities, clearly state, in a sentence or two, how your organization will achieve each objective. In other words, exactly what will your organization do to reach the objective? These are your methods.

4. Test the effectiveness of each method by asking, If the organization uses this method, is it realistic to expect the method to solve the problem?

5. Make sure you have not confused objectives and methods. Do any of your methods talk about *what* the program will do? If so, restate them so that they address *how* your organization will do it.

THINKING ABOUT NEXT STEPS

Identify three ideas for taking the next step. For example, answer these questions: What other methods can be used to achieve each objective? Who will be responsible for completing each of the listed activities?

WHEN YOU ARE READY TO MOVE ON

When you are ready to write your proposal, you will make a timeline of the beginning and ending dates of the various steps and activities you have identified, and you will list the resources (money, personnel, facilities, equipment) your organization will need to accomplish each of these tasks. You will use this information, along with the methods you have selected, to create a clear methods statement.

EXERCISE 5

■

LAYING THE GROUNDWORK FOR YOUR EVALUATION PLAN

■ ■ ■ ■

Exercise 5 will help you take the first steps toward showing a potential funder how you will measure the success of your project or program. It will help you decide how you will determine success, recognize what is and is not measurable, and begin to think about ways to evaluate the effectiveness and efficiency of your programs or projects. This will lay the groundwork for the evaluation plan section of your proposal.

ACTIVITY

1. Write down your project or program objectives from Exercise 3 and the corresponding methods from Exercise 4.

2. Talk with others in the organization or with colleagues about how your organization will define success. Think about the impact your program will need to have in order to be considered successful. Outline your thoughts here. Be specific. For example, if your organization is opening a soup kitchen, how many people will it need to serve over what time period for your program to be considered a success?

3. For each project, list the ways the organization will go about measuring its success. For example, will your organization keep statistics, interview the people served, use direct observation?

▨ *THINKING ABOUT NEXT STEPS*

What are three ideas you have for taking the next steps? For example, can you identify similar programs that have had success in a related area? Identify who in your organization will be responsible for making the evaluation assessments and for taking the evaluation plan to the appropriate level of detail. Where will you go to collect data to measure the success of the program?

▨ *WHEN YOU ARE READY TO MOVE ON*

When you are ready to write the evaluation plan for your proposal, you will need to go into more detail about what will be measured. Discuss with your board members, or with colleagues, how they have evaluated the success of other programs or projects they have implemented. You will use this information along with the work you have done in this exercise to create an effective evaluation plan.

EXERCISE 6

IDENTIFYING SOURCES FOR FUTURE FUNDING

■ ■ ■ ■ ■

Exercise 6 will help you take the first steps in building a case that your program can sustain itself financially once the grant period is over—that you have resources for future funding. This information is crucial. Foundations fund programs that can maintain themselves after the initial grant.

ACTIVITY

1. List your organization's existing fundraising programs.

2. Name five revenue-producing programs or events that other organizations have used successfully to raise funds.

3. List the revenue-producing programs or events of other organizations that could be appropriate for your organization. Then list the ones that are not appropriate but could be modified to fit.

4. Describe the new opportunities for future funding that the grant or your organization's new program or project might open up.

THINKING ABOUT NEXT STEPS

What are the next three things you could do? For example, discuss the pros and cons of each of your fundraising ideas with others in your organization or with colleagues. Brainstorm ideas for new sources of revenue, such as memberships drives, special fundraising events, or gift clubs.

WHEN YOU ARE READY TO MOVE ON

When you are ready to write your proposal, you will evaluate each fundraising idea and select those that will work best. These will become part of your proposal's future funding section.

EXERCISE 7

■

GETTING READY TO DEVELOP A BUDGET FOR YOUR PROJECT OR PROGRAM

■ ■ ■ ■

Answering the questions in Exercise 7 will help you set the stage for creating an accurate budget for your organization's proposed project or program. It is the first step in preparing a project proposal budget that shows how your organization will combine its resources and a funding agency's resources to form a cost-effective partnership.

ACTIVITY

1. All project and programs have associated expenses. Without filling in the dollar amounts, list as many categories of program expenses as you can. Some typical examples of expenses are salaries and benefits for program staff, supplies, equipment, travel expenses, rent, and printing.

2. Start thinking about how much each of your methods (from Exercise 4) will cost. List each method and its *approximate* cost. If you do not know these figures, where can you go to find out?

3. List revenue sources and amounts (other than the grant you are requesting). This information will help you determine what expenses your organization can cover and what expenses your organization will need a grant to cover.

4. The proposed budget will cover a specific time frame. This time frame is usually the length of the project. What length of time will your budget cover?

THINKING ABOUT NEXT STEPS

What are three to five ideas you have for taking the next steps? For example, how will you determine the various budget expenses? Is there a financial person in the organization who can help develop the budget? If not, who will take on this responsibility, and how will this person get the appropriate training?

WHEN YOU ARE READY TO MOVE ON

When you are ready to write your proposal, you will develop a budget like the sample on page 57. Discuss with the board whether any overhead expenses will be included in this proposed budget. Select a staff person or volunteer who will be responsible for gathering any required cost estimates. Think about whether you will need outside assistance to write or review the budget.

PART 2

RESURCES

■ ■ ■ ■ ■

The handy reference guides in Resource A give you a quick review of the material covered in the video, tips for each of the twelve elements of a grant proposal, and a sample of each element (information in square brackets identifies the key parts of each sample). Resources B and C offer tips on strategy and structure and the reasons some proposals get funded and some do not.

RESOURCE A

THE 12 KEY ELEMENTS OF A GRANT PROPOSAL

LIST OF KEY ELEMENTS

1. Cover letter
2. Title page
3. Table of contents
4. Summary
5. Introduction
6. Problem or need statement
7. Program objectives
8. Methods
9. Evaluation plan
10. Plans for future funding
11. Budget
12. Appendices

1. COVER LETTER

The cover letter is the first thing a potential funder is likely to read. It must engage the reader so he or she will read the rest of the proposal. An effective cover letter is personal, to the point, and concise. It includes these four basic elements:

1. Goals and objectives of the proposed project or program
2. Number of clients or other people to be served
3. Total amount of request
4. Length of program

It is not uncommon for a funder to read only the cover letter and then reject the proposal. Typically, a funder will reject a request on the basis of the cover letter when

1. The proposal is not in line with the foundation's mission.
2. The amount of the request exceeds the funding scope of the foundation.
3. The foundation has recently funded a similar proposal.

HOT TIP The cover letter is the first section of the proposal your funder will read. However, you will compose this letter *after* you have completed the other elements of the proposal.

Sample Cover Letter

Mr. George Goodman
Executive Director
The Good People's Foundation
100 First Street
Goodville, USA 11111

Dear Mr. Goodman:

The Friends of the Brisbane Library is submitting this proposal to the Good People's Foundation for $10,000 [*amount of request*] to implement a new library program: Friends of the Brisbane Library Home Delivery Service. This new program will enable homebound, physically impaired, and elderly residents to order circulating library materials for delivery to their homes [*stated goals and objectives of proposed program*].

The board of directors of the Friends believes this library home delivery program will provide 500 people [*number of clients or people served*] with an important service that gives them resources that would otherwise be inaccessible. The home delivery service will be initiated in July 2001 and will become an ongoing program of the library [*length of program*]. The Friends hope for your favorable response to our request for funding.

Our executive director, Joan Smith, will be contacting you within the next two weeks to schedule a meeting. Ms. Smith will provide you with more information about our proposed program and can answer any questions.

Sincerely,
John Doe
President, Board of Directors

■ 2. TITLE PAGE

The title page of a proposal must grab—and hold—the reader's attention. Along with the cover letter, it creates the reader's first impression of your proposal. It includes these six items:

1. Proposal title
2. Your organization's name
3. Program or project beginning and ending dates
4. Amount of funds requested
5. Project director's name, address, and telephone number
6. Agency director's name, address, and telephone number

An engaging title is vital to a successful grant proposal. For example, *Goldenville's New Home for the Arts* is less compelling than *Innovative Solutions for Goldenville's Needs in the Arts: The New Downtown Art Center and Emporium.* A powerful title can give your organization an edge on the competition and persuade the funder to put your request in the "to read" pile.

Spend time brainstorming ideas for the right title for your project or program.

Sample Title Page

Better Education
Through Better Nutrition

A Pilot Program to
Help Nutritionally Needy Children
in Jackson's Kindergarten Classrooms [*title*]

Proposed by
JACKSON FOOD BANK [*agency name*]

Project Dates . . . . . . September 5–June 11, 2000 [*beginning and ending dates*]
Request . . . . $500,000 [*amount of funds requested*]
Project Director . . . Carol Mason [*project director's name*]
Agency Director . . . Jean Davis [*agency director's name*]

JACKSON FOUNDATION
64 RAYMOND AVENUE
JACKSON, MI
PHONE: 601-555-0000
[*project and agency director's address and telephone number*]

▦ *3.* TABLE OF CONTENTS

The table of contents is an essential courtesy to the reader, offering him or her needed orientation, organization, and focus.

Sample Table of Contents

4. Summary

The summary (or abstract) is a succinct, clear synopsis of the project. It gives the funder a quick look at what the proposal will cover in more detail.

Keep this phrase in mind when writing the summary: short and sweet: *short* enough to be read quickly (a page or less is a good guideline), and *sweet* enough to interest potential funders and capture the proposal's essential points.

Your summary will

1. Identify your organization, and *briefly* give it credibility. (You will establish your organization's credibility more firmly in the introduction.)
2. State the problem or need.
3. List the program or project objectives.
4. Outline the methods.
5. List the amount of the request.

HOT TIP   Like the cover letter, the summary will be written *after* the rest of the proposal.

HOT TIP   Because the contact person at a foundation will often initially present just your summary to the foundation board, make sure it states your cause compellingly.

Sample Summary

The Action Mediation Center serves Smith County high school students. The mission of Action Mediation Center is to empower high school students to resolve their interpersonal conflicts.

Last year, the Action Mediation Center was recognized as The Mediation Program of the Year by the President's Council on Conflict Resolution. In recognition of the program's success, director Bill Smith was singled out for praise by the National Education Association [*identifies the agency and gives it credibility*].

Recognizing that Kelly High School has the highest incidence of on-campus physical violence in Smith County, the Action Mediation Center is proposing to create an ongoing mediation training program that will teach Kelly students the mediation skills needed to resolve conflicts. These students will in turn teach other students [*explains the methods*]. The purpose of this new program is to reduce conflicts and acts of violence on the campus of Kelly High School.

Violence in high schools is on the rise. According to *News Today*, acts of violence on high school campuses have increased more than 25 percent in the past ten years. Today's high school students need training to learn how to resolve conflicts without resorting to violent acts [*states the problem or need*]. A recent survey by *High School Today* magazine reports that high schools that have implemented the Action Mediation Center's conflict resolution program have reduced violent acts by 50 percent.

The objectives of the Kelly High School Mediation Program are twofold: (1) to teach Kelly students the skills they need to resolve interpersonal conflicts and (2) to reduce the number of physical altercations occurring on the Kelly High School campus [*lists the objective or objectives*].

Action Mediation Center members have served target populations for ten years, providing twenty participating high schools with quality mediation training services. The Kelly High School Mediation Program will expand the Action Mediation Center's efforts and give Kelly students much-needed training in conflict resolution skills.

First-year program costs are expected to be $50,000. This proposal is for $10,000 [*lists the amount of the request*]. Remaining funds for the new program will come from a grant from the Nation's Mediation Center, from other foundation sources, and from the Action Mediation Center's annual event.

5. Introduction

The introduction is your opportunity to establish your organization's credibility with the potential funder. The introduction should incorporate the following information:

1. A description of the grant applicant (your organization)
2. A list of your organization's aims and goals
3. A list of your organization's activities and achievements
4. Reliable statistics that document your organization's achievements
5. An explanation of the ways clients or others benefit from your organization's existence

Funders give money to projects that match the interests of the funding organization. The introduction is where you show how your organization's needs are allied with the stated interests of the funder.

HOT TIP

Introductions often also include a brief statement about the proposed project. In addition, you can include your organization's mission statement and information on how and why the organization was formed.

Sample Introduction

The Wildwood Dance Workshop was formed ten years ago as a 501(c)(3) nonprofit. The intent of this organization is to offer quality tap and ballet dance instruction for the children of the Wildwood community ages six to ten [*lists the aims and goals of the organization*].

When the Wildwood Dance Workshop first opened its doors, it filled an artistic void by being the first organization to offer dance lessons for the young people of the community. Since that time, 2,300 Wildwood youngsters have completed at least one of the workshop's twelve-week dance sessions [*description of the grant applicant*]. Each year the workshop provides Wildwood with a number of cultural events. Four times a year the workshop teams up with the Wildwood High School Band to present public performances that help fund the dance workshop. This past year's performances—*The Nutcracker, Wildwood's Spring Fling, Summertime Blues,* and *Twirly Birdies*—drew more than 3,000 audience members and raised $25,000.

During the workshop's first year of operation, *The Wildwood Gazette* called it "the best dance lesson value a parent could hope for." And for the past five years the *County Register* has listed the Wildwood Dance Workshop on its "Top 10 After School Activities for Kids" [*the organization's activities and achievements*].

The board of directors of the Wildwood Dance Workshop comprises former Wildwood students and other interested community members. The current board president is a former dance instructor with American Ballet Theater. The board meets bimonthly to review the workshop's efforts and discuss ways of coordinating its resources.

Two part-time instructors teach the dance classes and one part-time director coordinates the program and manages the fundraising efforts.

The Wildwood Dance Workshop's 2000 spring season had 125 students enrolled in the workshop's five classes, providing them with quality tap and ballet dance lessons. In 1999, 250 different boys and girls ages six to ten completed one or more of Wildwood's twelve-week dance classes [*reliable statistics that document achievements*].

Currently, children from households with incomes below the poverty line make up 10 percent of the total number of children living in Wildwood. Of the children currently participating in the dance workshop, only 2 percent are students from these low-income households. To address this underserved population, the Wildwood Dance Workshop will expand the scope of its operation by offering fifty economically disadvantaged children of Wildwood, ages six to ten, full scholarships for dance lessons [*an explanation of how clients benefit*].

6. Problem or Need Statement

The need statement answers these fundamental questions: Why have you put together the new project or program? What problem will it solve? What need will it fill? In this section you will

1. State the problem or need.
2. Show that your organization is not trying to accomplish the impossible.
3. Document the problem.

You can document the problem in a number of ways. For example, you can use one or more of these tools:

Statistics ("*x* millions of kids suffer from learning disabilities").

Surveys or questionnaires ("a recent survey on learning disabilities in children noted that one in three is likely to go undiagnosed").

Facts or predictions by authorities.

Results of interviews with client population.

Projections (showing for example that the problem is likely to worsen without your solution).

Statements quoted from newspapers or other published sources.

 Keep the need statement free from jargon and technical terms. Your goal is to communicate clearly with the potential funder.

Sample Need Statement

According to a recent census taken by the city of Thomasville, 18 percent of the city's population are senior citizens who are sixty years old or older. Professor John Smith of the Center for the Aging at St. Boniface University predicts that if current population trends continue, this number will increase to 25 percent within the next five years [*facts and prediction from an authority*]. Currently, more than two-thirds of these senior citizens do not own a car or are too ill or frail to avail themselves of public transportation.

The Daily Telegraph reports that more than half the senior residents of Thomasville live on a fixed income that is below the federal poverty line and more than 16 percent exist on their Social Security payments alone. In the past two years free door-to-door transportation services for disadvantaged seniors have been drastically cut and in many cases eliminated because of loss of funding at the county and state levels [*statistics, quoted from a newspaper report*].

This loss of transportation services has caused untold hardship for many seniors. For example, Mr. Smith (a retired, eighty-three-year-old railroad worker) had been using the county-funded transportation system to go back and forth for his weekly doctor's appointment. This appointment is vital to Mr. Smith's good health because he must have his medication monitored weekly. When the county cut the transportation program last year, Mr. Smith was unable to keep his weekly appointment and suffered severe medical complications [*interview with client population*].

Daniel Johnson, M.D., of the State Medical Board, predicts that "the lack of door-to-door transportation for seniors will cause countless elderly patients to forego medical treatment, putting them at serious medical risk." The need to provide Thomasville seniors with a door-to-door transportation service is overwhelming [*projection of need*]. A recent survey of Blanchard County residents revealed that 33 percent of the seniors surveyed have missed one or more doctor's appointments since the door-to-door transportation services were cut last year [*survey information*].

The nonprofit Seniors' Transport Organization has been providing quality, accident-free transportation services for the elderly adults of the cities of Maryville, Stanton, and Blaine in Blanchard County for more than twenty years. Expanding our services into Thomasville is a cost-effective way to provide transportation services for the underserved, elderly residents of this community.

7. PROGRAM OBJECTIVES

After you state the need—or *why* you are proposing this program—the next step is to tell the funder *what* your organization is going to do about it. This is your program objective (or objectives). When determining an objective, your operative word is *to*. The program's objective is *to* do something very specific that will solve a problem or satisfy a need.

The objective must be realistic, should not be overblown, and must be confined to what could conceivably be accomplished by your organization with its resources. "To stop children in the tri-county area from going to bed hungry" is an example of an objective that an organization might reasonably accomplish. "To stop children all over the world from going to bed hungry" is not.

HOT TIP

A fundable objective must reflect a result that can be quantified. It should be time sensitive. The change it effects must be measurable. (If there is no way to measure the change produced, reconsider the objective.)

Sample Objectives

A Pet Adoption Program

The objective of Shasta Pet Rescue is to find good homes for 100 abandoned dogs and cats in Door County each year, reducing the need for euthanasia of abandoned animals and protecting the public from potentially dangerous strays.

A High School Mediation Program

The objective of the Kelly High School Mediation Program is to teach Kelly students the skills they need to resolve interpersonal conflicts and to decrease violent acts on campus by 30 percent within three years.

A Children's Dance Workshop

The objective of the Wildwood Dance Workshop is to give fifty economically disadvantaged children of Wildwood, ages six to ten, free dance lessons each year, offering them a safe, enriching after-school activity.

A Library Home Delivery Program

The objective of the Friends of the Brisbane Library Home Delivery Service is to provide all homebound Brisbane residents with permanent access to the library's circulating materials, helping them lead fuller lives and avoid feelings of isolation and loneliness.

A Children's Fitness Program

The objective of Kids Get Fit is to get 80 percent of Port Charles children ages eight to thirteen to meet the President's Guidelines for physical fitness within two years.

A Civic Action Program

The objective of the Save Green Mountain organization is to make Green Mountain a part of the statewide park system, preserving it as a natural resource for the Green Mountain community and for the public at large.

8. METHODS

Once you have established *why* your organization's project is necessary and *what* your organization is going to do about it, you need to tell the funder *how* your organization will meet the need and accomplish the objective (or objectives). Your organization may have several methods for accomplishing any one objective. However, all methods should be developed from a specific objective.

It is important to delineate each method and the reasons why it was selected. You should be able to show that each method chosen is less time consuming, less costly, and more effective than other methods and that it has a proven track record.

After your organization determines each method, it will need to set out a timeline for putting that method to work. What does your organization expect to accomplish with this method in a year or two or three? How long will each step take?

Do not confuse methods with objectives. An objective describes a result. A method is the way you will accomplish that result.

Sample Methods

Note that each of the following two methods is developed from the objective and that each timeline is developed from the method.

Objective

The goal of the Wildwood Dance Workshop is to offer fifty economically disadvantaged children of Wildwood, ages six to ten, free dance lessons each year, offering them a safe, enriching after-school activity.

Method

Wildwood Dance Workshop will establish a scholarship program and create a panel to screen applicants for eligibility.

Timeline

June 2002	Wildwood Dance Workshop establishes first scholarship program.
July 2002	Scholarship panel reviews applicants and selects scholarship winners.
September 2002	First group of scholarship winners begins dance classes.
January 2002	Workshop publishes first progress report.

Objective

The goal of the Friends of the Brisbane Library Home Delivery Service is to provide all homebound Brisbane residents with permanent access to the library's circulating materials, helping them lead fuller lives and avoid feelings of isolation and loneliness.

Method

Using library volunteers we will set up a program for home delivery, create a communications method, and notify residents of the home delivery service.

Timeline

January 2002	Program for library home delivery is put in place.
February 2002	Delivery telephone hot-line is installed at library.
March 2002	All Brisbane residents are notified by mail of new home delivery service.
July 2002	Program's first progress report is issued.

9. *EVALUATION PLAN*

After you have shown the foundation what your organization will do and how your organization will do it, you need to show this potential funder how your organization will measure the success of the program or project—so the foundation knows that if it decides to give money to your organization, it will be able to see later whether it made a good investment. A good evaluation plan will include these elements:

1. A strategy for measuring the success of achieving objectives.

2. An explanation of the criteria used to measure success.

3. Statements quoted from experts.

4. Comparisons to similar programs.

A recent trend in evaluations is that funders are demanding clearly defined outcomes. An *outcome* is the significant change a program makes or hopes to make in the community. For example, evaluation might establish this specific outcome of an educational program that helps people find employment: "of the twenty-five people who took all five classes offered and passed them all, 80 percent were hired in less than six months."

HOT TIP

Make sure the evaluation portion of your proposal answers these questions: How will your organization determine if the program is a success? What will be measured? What information will be collected? Who will be responsible for the assessment? Also note that outcomes are often integrated into the objectives section of the proposal and that the evaluation section then builds on these outcomes.

Sample Evaluation Criteria

Developing an evaluation plan is an in-depth and involved process. Here are some samples of the first step in this process—defining the criteria that will determine whether a program is a success. When you are ready to write your organization's proposal, you will integrate similar criteria into the evaluation plan.

A Pet Adoption Program

If 50 percent of the adoptable pets are adopted, the program will be deemed a success.

A Library Home Delivery Program

If, over a one-year period, volunteers from the Friends of the Brisbane Library deliver 80 percent of the materials requested by elderly, disabled, or homebound library patrons, the program will be called a success.

A Historical Walking Tour of Charleston

If, by year-end, the tours increase attendance by 50 percent from the initial start-up, the program will be determined a success.

A Children's Dance Workshop

If 75 percent of the low-income children enrolled complete the six-week program, the dance workshop scholarship program will be considered a success.

10. PLANS FOR FUTURE FUNDING

The future funding section of your proposal tells the funder how your organization will continue to support the program or project after the grant. Will the program need more funds after the initial funding? Will the program be able to sustain itself? It is important to build a persuasive case that the program can be sustained without future grant support.

HOT TIP

It is a mistake to generalize about future funding! Nonspecific statements—such as, "Our organization has plans to raise money from a variety of sources"—will raise a red flag for foundations.

Sample Future Funding Plan

The Friends of the Brisbane Library Home Delivery Program will receive ongoing funding from the Friends' annual book sale. In the past five years the book sale has annually generated more than $2,000 in revenue. In addition to these monies, the board of directors will increase the unrestricted funds available for the delivery program through a Valentine's Day direct-mail campaign, which in 1999 raised more than $3,000. Also, a percentage of the annual membership dues will go to fund the home delivery program. The Friends' membership has a history of growth, increasing 20 percent every year for the past ten years. The board also plans to support the delivery program with funds raised from the sale of Friends of the Brisbane Library tote bags. Based on information about tote sales from other Friends organizations in the area, it is projected that the first year's sale of the tote bags will generate $2,000.

11. BUDGET

The project proposal budget shows the funder how your organization's money and the funder's money will be used together to fund the project. It tells the funder that its money is well leveraged. The budget portion of the proposal also gives the funder much-needed insight into the overall expenses of your organization.

There are two types of budgets: an *operating budget,* which covers the finances for everything the organization does on an annual basis, and a *project budget,* which covers only the finances for a single project or program. Sometimes an organization's operating budget is the same as the budget for the project or program that needs funding. When it is not, you must obtain or if necessary create a separate project budget.

HOT TIP Often a funder will want to know exactly where the revenue will come from to cover the organization's share of the program expenses. Be prepared to provide this information.

The sample budget shown here is a three-part vertical drop budget. Read from left to right, it reveals the structure of a proposed funding partnership. The left-hand column shows the organization's contribution in each expense category, the center column shows the foundation's contribution, and the right-hand column shows the total amount. Note that many foundations will not fund capital expenses, such as computers or cellular phones.

Sample Three-Part Vertical Drop Budget

	Our Contribution	Foundation Contribution	Total Budget
Personnel			
Direct costs			
Project director salary	$20,000	$35,000	$55,000
Support staff salaries	25,000	—	25,000
Indirect costs	*[Some organizations, usually governmental agencies, will fund indirect costs such as health benefits, pension funds, and Social Security costs.]*		
Health benefits	7,000	—	7,000
Space			
Cost per square foot	8,000	4,000	12,000
Utilities	1,200	—	1,200
Telephones	800	—	800
Equipment			
Furniture	1,500	—	1,500
Telephones	1,000	—	1,000
Computers	1,200	1,200	2,400
Faxes	800	—	800
Copiers	900	—	900
Travel	*[This section is needed when organization members must travel to reach specific populations or attend grant-related meetings.]*		
Transportation	5,000	2,000	7,000
Meals	800	—	800
Lodging	1,600	600	2,200
Supplies	*[The cost of supplies is absorbed by the organization and should be listed in columns one and three only.]*		
Paper	600	—	600
Light bulbs	—	—	—
Pens and pencils	50	—	50
Dissemination	*[This section is included when the organization publishes a report.]*		
Report printing	1,800	1,800	3,600
Report postage	700	350	1,050
GRAND TOTALS	$77,950	$44,950	$122,900

12. APPENDICES

The appendices are the final part of the grant proposal. They are the place for background information and any additional information you think the funder may want to see. The funder will probably read only the appendices of particular interest to him or her. So state clearly at the appropriate points in the body of your proposal that more information on a topic is available in an appendix (for example, "see Appendix B for a list of current board of directors members").

The appendices may contain one or more of these items:

1. Resumes of the project director and agency director
2. List of board of directors members
3. News articles about the organization or the need
4. Letters of recommendation
5. Statistical data
6. Organization's brochure
7. Fact sheets
8. Organization's mission statement
9. Organization's strategic plan
10. List of past grants to the organization
11. Organization's current operating budget
12. Copy of organization's newsletter
13. Organization's most recent W-9 form
14. Evidence of organization's nonprofit status
15. Description of organization's purpose
16. State proclamation about organization
17. Organization's articles of incorporation
18. Organization's current bylaws

On the first page of the appendices, provide a mini-table of contents that lists each appendix.

RESOURCE B

SOME TIPS ON
STRATEGY AND STRUCTURE

▪ ▪ ▪ ▪ ▪

To give your grant proposal that all-important competitive edge, create reader-friendly text. Where appropriate, use headers and lists with numbers or bullets. Well-crafted declarative sentences and short paragraphs invite the reader to make his or her way logically and effortlessly down the page and through to the end of the proposal. Use double spacing only if the funder requests it. In addition

- Use language to your best advantage. Select words that dramatize your proposal.

- Use a quotation from a notable source if it will add interest and drama to your proposal.

- Never use six words when two will do. Funders appreciate proposals that are stylistically economical.

- Do not use exaggerations or subjective assertions. They compromise your organization's position and reduce its competitive effectiveness.

- Be sure the proposal speaks to its audience. Funders and other outsiders may not understand the language and culture of your organization. Before submitting a proposal, test it. Ask qualified persons outside your organization to evaluate *what* the proposal says about the organization and *how* it is said. Is the proposal clear, persuasive, and motivational?

- Request an amount within the funder's typical funding range. If a foundation has a history of funding grants from

$10,000 to $25,000, do not ask for more or less than those amounts (unless directed otherwise by your funder).

- *Never send out a generic proposal. Always customize the proposal to the funder.*

RESOURCE C

WHY SOME PROPOSALS GET FUNDED AND SOME DO NOT

As you prepare to write your organization's grant proposal, consider these reasons why funders accept and reject proposals.

WHY PROPOSALS GET FUNDED

Foundations and other funders generally select an organization's project or program for funding because

- It targets an underserved population.
- It provides a service that is not currently available.
- It represents a collaboration of nonprofits working together to provide the service.
- It brings something new and creative to the resolution of a need or problem.

Many foundations are highly accessible and welcome your questions. You can talk to their representatives by telephone, and they will assist you in the process of applying for funds.

WHY SOME PROPOSALS GET REJECTED

Grant proposals are most often rejected because

- The project is outside the funder's mission.
- The proposal missed the funder's deadline.

- The project's methods are not clearly defined.
- The amount requested is outside the foundation's funding limits.
- The project duplicates programs already available elsewhere.
- The proposal is poorly written and improperly documented.
- The proposal is well written and the project is worthy, but the funds are not available. No foundation has the resources to respond favorably to all requests.

CONCLUSION

■

WHERE DO YOU GO FROM HERE?

■ ■ ■ ■ ■

Now that you have learned about the basic elements of a grant proposal and have begun to think like a grantwriter, you are ready to move on to write your grant proposal. Using the information in the video and the background work you have done in this workbook, you have started down the path to writing successful grant proposals.

The grant money is there for the asking. By law, foundations must give away 5 percent of their assets every year. The very reason foundations exist is to provide funding for the most qualified nonprofits. A successful proposal takes time and preparation, but it can reap enormous financial rewards for your organization.

N O T E S

NOTES

NOTES